The Magic Money Formula:

Get What You Want Now through Money Mindset Makeover, Law of Attraction, and the Magic Money Formula!

Samantha A. Gregory

© 2016-2021 Samantha Gregory

All rights reserved. No part of this book may be copied or reproduced via audio, video, or any other means without the express written consent of the author.

Disclaimer: This book is for informational purposes only. No part of this work may be construed as medical, psychological, or financial advice. Apply the information responsibly and at your own risk.

Table of Contents

What is Manifestation or Manifesting?	4
Part 1 - Storytime: How I manifested $9k in less than 9 days	7
Manifesting Much More than Money!	10
Manifesting A Man (Photos)	11
Manifesting More Miracles (House)	12
Part 2 - The Goal Writing Habit	15
The 5-Step Magic Money Manifestation Formula	16
Part 3 - Other Manifestation Techniques	18
Spoken Manifestation	18
Written Manifestation	20
Pictures/Vision Board Manifestation	22
Scripting Manifestation	23
Two-Cup Manifestation	25
Mirror Manifesting	26
EFT Manifestation	28
Feeling it Real is the Secret	30
Final Thoughts	31
Cultivate Your Confidence	31
Obey the Law of Giving and Receiving	31
The ABCs of Prayer	32
Appendix A - Scripting Worksheets	35
55 x 5 Worksheet	35
33 x 3 Worksheet	38
Appendix B - Sexy Good Goals Worksheet	40

Imagine thinking about what you want and taking specific action that doesn't require blood, sweat or tears to get it. How awesome would that be? What if you could get anything you wanted now using a basic formula like the one below?

I've used this formula and I've gotten money, homes, cars, jobs, vacations, and basically anything I want. You might think it's luck or that I have a rich family. None of that is true. I came from humble family beginnings. Both my parents, my grandparents, and my great-grandparents were poor growing up. They were working class people who struggled to survive.

I struggled to survive for a while but then I decided I wanted to get off the survival and struggle train. I wanted more for my life and I was determined to have it. That began my quest to find the answer to create a better life for myself and family.

I came across the book The Science of Getting Rich which started my journey into money manifestation. In this book you will learn what I learned about manifesting what you want through a simple formula that I call:

The Magic Money Formula

SR +   PF +   RG   = M

Specific **R**equest + **P**ositive **F**eelings + **R**adical **G**ratitude = **Manifestation**

What is Manifestation or Manifesting?

When people hear the word manifest, manifestation, or manifesting, all kinds of thoughts and ideas jump around in their heads. For some it is a kind of religious practice, for others it sounds like woo-woo magical stuff that is mysterious and suspect. It's often associated with the Law of Attraction and *The Secret*. It seems to be all the things that are wrapped in mystery and takes special skills to make happen.

For me, manifesting is about using decisive thoughts and feelings to bring the things I desire into my physical world. If you ask 10 different people you will get 10 different answers. In essence, manifesting is a personal thing. After you read this book and put the techniques into practice you will likely have your own definition of the word.

We are all manifestors whether we understand what that means or believe is possible. Everything we see, touch, hear, taste, or feel is a manifestation of our thoughts and feelings. When I say "our," I mean people on this planet both past and present.

It doesn't matter if what we are experiencing is good or bad, it is all a manifestation that began in the mind.

You could say the mind and manifestation are twins. We can't see our mind but we know it is there. We can think, make our bodies move, taste certain things, and hear select sounds. We can make most things happen with a thought. It's basic and everyone can do it. We control the physical movement, the experience, and the outcome.

What if we could control other things like money, health, love? Seems impossible because we are told we have to work hard for the things we want but is that really true? What if it were effortless to have the things we desire? What if just by deciding we want something, imagining it were true, and feeling excitement and gratitude about it, it just happened? Would that freak you out or make you do cartwheels?

I'm here to tell you it is absolutely true! I'm a witness and in the next few pages I'm going to share my manifestation experiences. Then I'm going to share how you can do what I did. I'm even going to go a few steps further and share the seven methods I've used to manifest different things in my life at different times.

A person looking outside would assume I'm lucky because I always seem to get what I want; prime jobs, amazing pay, great kids, trips, cars, and basically anything I want. It's not luck though. It is the power of manifestation.

Here's a secret. Manifestation is really just prayer, belief, and connection with God/Source except on steroids! He is the source of EVERYTHING and wants us to have whatever we desire but we have to allow it to manifest and flow into our physical space. Keep reading to find out how I manifest what I want and how you can too!

Broke, Busted, and Disgusted
A few years ago I was broke and needed money to cover my rent and other expenses. I was not getting assignments on my job and other contracts had dried up. I had to request an extension on all my bills.

I was beginning to feel desperate but I knew desperation would do no good. Despite all the amazing things I had going on, it was not enough from a skill and talent point of view to meet my financial obligations. It seemed nothing I did was working or at least not working on time.

I decided to pray about it and keep doing what I was doing in my normal routine. I wrote blog posts. I looked for work. I sent out newsletters. I connected with family and friends. Ironically, I didn't ask or want to ask any of them for help. Chalk it up to my stubborn pride...

My thinking was to do all I could to get the money I needed for my expenses. **I stopped myself from doing extraordinary things to force the money to come.** The striving and work hard mentality was not for me this time. I knew I needed to relax and attract the money I wanted. I would need a miracle and despite all odds I had to believe a miracle *could* happen. I kept praying and applying my faith as much as possible.

A Solution I Could Try

One day I was online and came across a free Udemy course that was about goal setting. The instructor described the technique he used to set goals and reach them in a short time. I thought about my situation and decided it wouldn't hurt to set a money goal using this technique.

I watched the training again and did what it said step by step. The simplicity of it was too good to be true, but the consistency was important if it was to work.

I later learned this technique is called **Scripting**, the practice of writing a scripted statement repeatedly in future tense over a course of a few days. This exercise plants the thought in your subconscious mind which goes to work finding the solution or bringing the specific request into manifestation.

Part 1 - Storytime: How I manifested $9k in less than 9 days

I decided how much I needed and the date by which I needed it.

I took a **notebook** and **wrote** a future goal statement. This means I wrote my specific request as if it were already fulfilled.

I wrote my specific as follows:
"On January 20, I receive **$2k or better** to pay my rent and bills. Yes!"

Here is how I started writing the specific request:

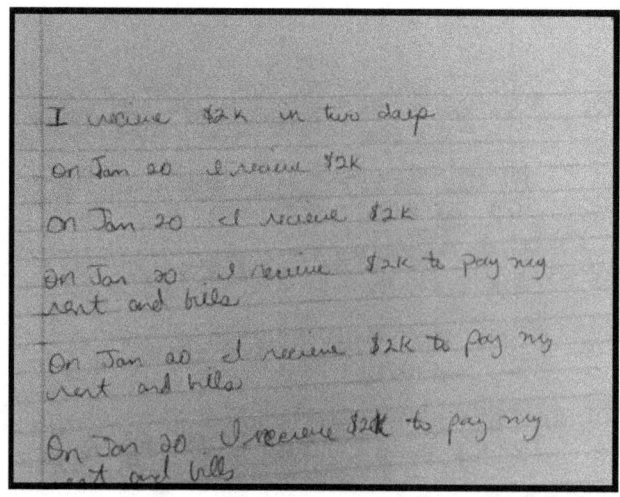

It was a rough start; quite disjointed but it became clearer as I kept working with it. I finally **decided what I wanted** and could **write it with amazing clarity** in my specific request.

Here is how I finished it:

I wrote my specific request on the front and back of notebook paper **every day for two days**; morning and evening. My hand was tired but my heart was determined.

The Day of Reckoning
On the 20th, I had the full expectation that I would receive the money I needed to pay my rent and bills. The day went on without any money being deposited into my bank or PayPal account, no one stopped by to give me cash, and a check did not come in the mail. I was not discouraged because the day was not over.

I sat down to read my mail and almost tossed an envelope aside from my retirement company. I opened the envelope and my heart sank as I looked at the numbers. It said I had a $0 balance! I began running through all the financial news of the day and week. I had heard nothing of a financial fall out or melt down. How could I not have money in my retirement account!?!?!

Fortunately I read closer and it said the account had been moved to a new service so all my money had been transferred. Whew!

The Money Manifested!!!
I looked through the rest of my mail and saw the envelope from the new retirement company. I opened it and saw the **balance was just under $10k**! I couldn't believe it but I did believe it. I hadn't looked at my retirement balance in a long time so I didn't know how much was there. It had been years since I contributed but it kept up a steady growth.

I needed $2k for my bills but I manifested way more! How? In my specific request I said I wanted $2k+. **The "+" sign was the key to manifesting more**. Requesting "two thousand or more" took the limitations off of what I could have. I also believe it is because God always gives "exceedingly and abundantly more than I could ask or think"!

Most would argue and say that money was for retirement and shouldn't be touched but I've never been one for strict convention. I was experiencing a hardship that qualified for withdrawal so I requested it. The money came from a source that I needed to tap into at the time. I had no thought of that account or money at any time during my temporary crisis up until that moment. If I had, it would not be a miracle for me. I was walking in blind faith during that time, so the retirement money was my miracle.

When I made the call I asked as many questions as I could. I understood the risks and penalties I would receive so I went ahead with the transaction. I completed the paperwork and sent it back. The lady on the phone was super nice and everything was processed in three days! My previous retirement company would have made me jump through hoops to get the money so the change in companies was a blessing. Within 3 days the money I requested was deposited into my bank account.

… And that is my story of how I manifested $9k in less than 9 days.

I followed certain simple principles that resulted in a fantastic windfall. I think my experience is unusual because the average person would have thought it too simplistic and even ridiculous. But simple faith and perseverance made all the difference. Some would say it was a fluke or a coincidence but I have proof that it's not. I manifested a new home and a man too using the same formula. Here is the evidence...

Manifesting Much More than Money!

Manifesting A Man

A few days after I received my money manifestation I wrote a specific request for a man. I wrote:

"Within one month I meet and begin a relationship with the man who will be my best friend/partner/husband. Yes!"

I wrote 11 pages of that specific request! I was serious and I did begin a relationship within a month of writing the request with a man I dated for a year. We started dating on February 14, 2015, to be exact.

Here are the notebook pages I wrote my specific request for a man on. Again, I had kind of a rough start deciding exactly what I wanted, but I quickly gained clarity. My hand was very tired from writing so much but I knew what I wanted.

Manifesting A Man (Photos)

1/23/16

and begin a relationship
I meet the man who will become my best friend/partner/husband in one month

I meet and begin a relationship with the man who will become my best friend/partner/husband

I meet and begin a relationship with the man who will become my BFPH

I meet and begin a relationship with the man who will become my best friend/partner/husband

Within one month I meet and begin a relationship with the man who will become my BFPH

Within one month I meet and begin a relationship with the man who will become my BFPH / yes

Manifesting More Miracles (House)

I wrote another specific request that I would find my dream house by June 30, 2015. I moved into my dream house as described by August 1, 2015!

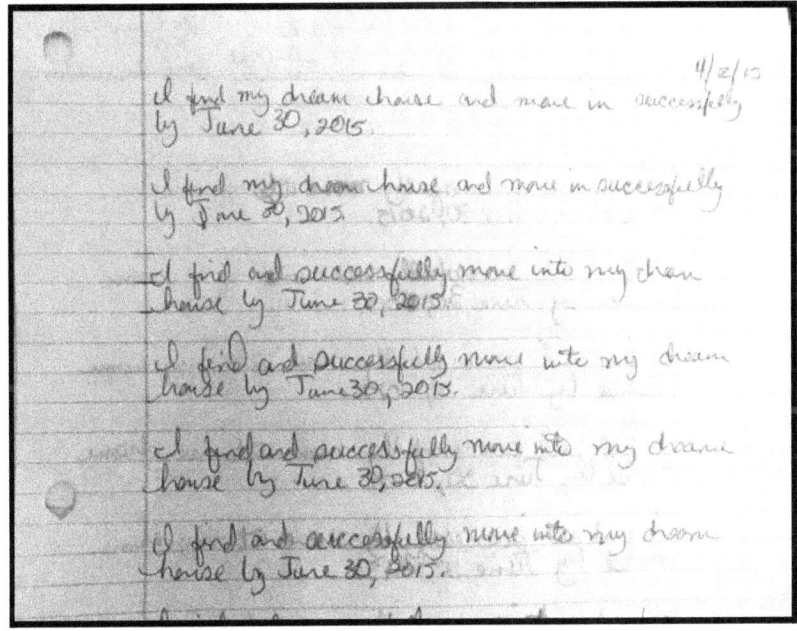

Here is a description of the kind of house I wanted to manifest:

An affordable, modern home with 4 bedrooms, 3 baths, 2-car garage, Porch/patio/deck, Basement, semi-secluded, quiet neighborhood, kind neighbors, convenient to stores, large master bedroom/bathroom/closet, hardwood floors, chocolate/black cabinets, stainless steel appliances, office.

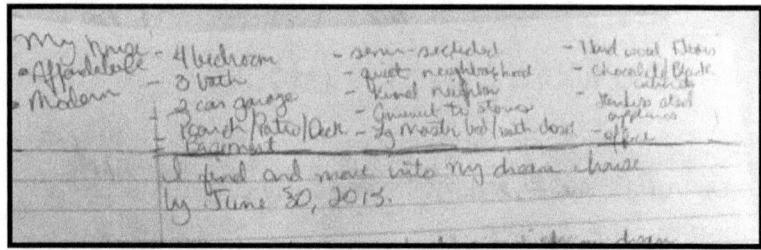

I was very specific about what I wanted and I got everything except the cabinets, appliances, and floor types I wrote down. However, my carpet was brand new and perfect for high traffic without looking terrible after wear and tear. I am super excited about that! On top of that I got two decks in the back of the house.

When I saw the house I knew it was for me. I basically told the landlord this was my house. The deposit was less than half of the rent amount which allowed me to hire a moving company to do all the heavy lifting and have an easier move.

I also wrote a specific request that my move would go smoothly and I'd get my full deposit back. The move went well and I got over half my deposit back. I accepted this and moved on to enjoy my new place.

Often we get more or better than what we asked for. Always be open to bigger and better outcomes. We can be specific but we don't have to be rigid. When we are flexible in our requests we get more than we can imagine or think! I think that is very exciting because God/Source wants the best for us and will give us everything we desire (and more) when we ask.

7/28/5

My move goes smoothly and miracle follows miracle. I get my entire deposit back.

My move goes smoothly, I get my full deposit back, and miracle follows miracle.

My move goes smoothly, I get my full deposit back, and miracle follows miracle.

My move goes smoothly on Friday, I get my full deposit back, and miracle follows miracle.

My move goes smoothly on Friday, I get my full deposit back, and miracle follows

My House Manifested (Photos)

Part 2 - The Goal Writing Habit

My goals have been manifested in amazing ways for years. It is not because I'm any more special than you are. I simply found a method that works for me. Writing down my goals has always been a part of my life.

I've done it for over 20 years starting after I read Steven Covey's, *The 7 Habits of Highly Effective People*, when my daughter was a year old. She is now in her twenties. I also read, *Write It Down Make it Happen*, a wonderful book that explains why writing your goals, dreams, and lists make what you want happen as if by magic.

My First Goals List
I wrote my first list of goals on a scrap piece of paper. I guess back then they were more like wishes. I put the list in my desk drawer and forgot about it. The biggest goal I had at the time was to make a $25k salary a year. Back then that was a lot of money to me.

About a year or so later I found the list and saw that over half of my wishes came true! Even the amount of money I wanted to make. From the time I made the list to when I came across it again, I had gotten a new, higher paying job making about $21k and child support brought me up to $25k.

I was hooked on setting goals after that. I didn't do it as consistently as I probably should have but each time I did amazing things happened.

I began telling anyone who would listen to start writing down their goals. Some people listened and others didn't. The ones who listened came back and told me how my advice worked for them. They'd write their goals and they all manifested for them. The ones who didn't listen are basically in the same place.

The Magic Behind Manifesting is...
Is there some kind of voodoo magic in writing your goals? Not the kind of magic born out of negativity but born from positive energy. What happens when you write your goals is you are making a statement of commitment just by writing what you want.

Your dream is no longer floating around in your head like all your wishes do. It becomes real to you (and God) that this is what you truly want. You have committed it to paper so it is pretty serious. If all it takes to reach your goals is writing it down, how much more powerful is it to write it down and put a date to it? Be specific about it? Write it repeatedly every day?

My method for manifesting $9k in less than 9 days is evidence of this. My entire focus was on the goal when I wrote it over and over for days until I got it. My brain went to work to find answers. **The universe conspired with me to manifest it because I was clear about it.** I was committed to it. I believed I should have it.

But the biggest and most important detail is that **I DECIDED what I wanted**. Until I made the decision, everything else was just a million pieces of a puzzle waiting to be brought together for a purpose.

So how do you manifest money, a house, or a man? Follow my 5-step formula below!

The 5-Step Magic Money Manifestation Formula

Here is a 5-step formula that I learned:

1. **Declutter your mind and space** - Clear your mind through meditation and soothing music. Clear your space by removing clutter, making your bed, cleaning up, and/ or organizing your stuff.

2. **Decide exactly what you want** - Get crystal clear on what you want to attract. A confused mind cannot focus so be sure about what you want and when you want it.

3. **Surround yourself with positivity** - Abundance cannot manifest in a negative space. Your mind, your words, your feelings, your heart must all be in a positive space. Do not allow any negativity to enter your surroundings. Consistent positive feelings accelerate the results.

4. **Take inspired action** - For this exercise, the inspired action is writing your specific request over and over. As you write, you cannot help but be

inspired to take certain action that will lead you to your goal.

5. **Receive** - When your goal manifests receive it with a grateful heart. Rejoice that your specific request has been answered then tell someone about your blessings.

The specific Scripting technique I used is as follows:

- ❏ Get clear about what you want
- ❏ Get a notebook and pen
- ❏ Formulate a specific, date driven goal statement
- ❏ Write the specific request repeatedly on the front and back of the paper
- ❏ Repeat this action each day until your goal is reached or until it feels okay to stop because your brain has received the message
- ❏ Watch for the signs and take inspired action
- ❏ Be radically thankful for receiving your specific request and tell someone about your blessing

I cannot guarantee that your experience will be like mine, but I am sure you will have wild success if you will give the formula a try. Follow the steps. Start with something small at first then work your way up to bigger things. The key is to start.

Remember the basic magic money formula:

$$SR + PF + RG = M$$

Part 3 - Other Manifestation Techniques

There are other manifestation techniques you can use to get what you want sooner than later. Here are the seven methods I've personally used that I think you would also benefit from as well.

Spoken Manifestation

Your words have power. One of my favorite authors, Florence Scovel Shinn, wrote the book, *Your Word is Your Wand*. In it she explains how much power your words have. We say words all day every day. We speak our destiny and future into existence day after day, week after week, month after month, and year after year.

Where you are today is a result of the words you spoke in the past. If you really sit down and think about it, you will see how what you said last week, last month, last year, or five years ago has become a reality for you. If you speak negative words about your life and situation, even about other people, those words come to life. If you are still in a bad situation at work, at home, with your health, with your money, take a look at the words you are speaking. Are they positive words or are they negative words? Are you complaining, or optimistic? Do you speak about the circumstances you see or the future you want?

It may sound too simple or too woo woo, but I promise you, it is simply a law of life and nature. You were created to be a creator. Your words create things. The Good Book (Bible) says your words will not return empty. What you sow (say) is what you will reap (see).

How do you use your words to create a future you deeply desire in your heart? I'm glad you asked and I'm happy to answer! Everyday when I wake up I say, "Today is a wonderful day!" Sounds simple right but guess what? When I say those words, I have a wonderful day. It doesn't mean I don't have challenges or irritations, but I don't allow those things to ruin my day. I have decided I'm in control of the outcome simply because I said my day is wonderful. Notice I didn't day, "Today **will** be a wonderful day." I said it *IS* a wonderful day. Right now and in every moment that comes.

The word "will" is an okay word but it is now powerful enough for what I want. The word "is" denotes present tense. It is definite and emphatic. It is a powerful command. Did you know you have that kind of power? I'm sure no one has ever told you that. From age two years old you have been told, "No" millions of times. You have been made powerless and your energetic words have been demagnetized. Today I'm giving you your power back. Your words, your thoughts, your will is powerful.

Here is something else you need to know about speaking words. You must speak them out loud. Why? Because words have energy and they vibrate in the atmosphere. They trigger things to start happening. Haven't you noticed how you feel when you sing and dance. You feel great! When you tell someone you love them they light up. When you say angry words to someone they are crushed.

The nursery rhyme, "sticks and stones may break my bones but words will never hurt me!" is false. Words have power to build up or tear down both others and you. What words do you speak to yourself? Do you call yourself names like, dummy, stupid, worthless, etc.? Those words have a very low, detrimental vibration. They hurt you and others. Don't use them. Use your power for good, not evil.

Don't sin against yourself by speaking low vibe words. Instead bless yourself with high vibe words; beautiful, smart, kind, clever, worthy, lovable. Speak them to yourself and to others. Compliment others. Speak words that heal not words that harm.

When my children were teens I spoke words about them for a future that was wonderful. I spoke blessings over them for good health, love, wealth, and perfect self-expression. I spoke these words because I know how powerful my words are. I spoke wisdom and favor from God and men. I spoke success over them. I spoke good over their lives. The awesome thing is I've already started seeing this good happen in their lives.

Speaking has power which means you have the power to change your life through your words. You talk daily to yourself and to others. Begin changing your words to match the future you want to see for your life. Create a daily habit of saying, "Today is a wonderful day!" When you do this you will notice that the number of bad days are few and far between the amazing days you have.

Declarations/Mantras/Affirmations

This is a category of speaking things into existence through repetitive words and phrases. Declaring is the term found in the religious arena. Mantras is the term found in the spiritual arena. Affirmations is the term used in the self-help or business arena. No matter what term you use, repeating words and phrases with high vibration feelings impresses your desires into your subconscious mind. Things happen because the words are spoken aloud. Write your words or phrases on your mirror, on sticky notes, or anywhere you will see it on a daily basis. Take it a step further and record your declarations, mantras, and affirmations then listen to it at night before bed. Listening to the spoken word is another way to get the idea into your subconscious to manifest your desires.

Another method I use to manifest a desire is to create a password phrase that I type every time I log into my computer. Just think how many times you log in at work. Typing your mantra each time deepens the impression on your subconscious mind. Try it to see what happens.

Your passphrase could look something like this to ensure it is secure:

Iget$1k2day! = I get $1000 today!

This is a secure and compliant password that is also a mantra.

Your Turn: Try to come up with your own then change your computer and/or account passwords to it.

Written Manifestation

Letter Writing

Writing a letter as a means to manifest what you want is a powerful technique to use. The very act of writing is an act of commitment to seeing your desire or wish fulfilled. Similar to writing goals, writing a letter is putting pen to paper which gets the vision of what you want out of your head and on the page.

How can writing a letter work? If you have ever gotten a letter/email from someone you care about you know how it makes you feel. When you write a letter you evoke high vibration feelings. You are hopeful, you are feeling good. You are memorializing the sentiments you feel.

What should your letter say? Basically, you are writing a letter to yourself or someone describing how the thing you want manifested. If you want a new car, you are writing as if you already got the car and describing how you got the car as well as the color, style, and how it drives. Your letter is a detailed account of the thing you manifested even though you don't have it in the physical realm yet. You don't include how you got it necessarily, but that you have it and how it feels.

You can write a letter about anything you want to manifest. You can write every day or every week. Whenever you feel inspired simply write. It can be a paragraph or several pages. The key is to write about how you feel and the details of the things you desire.

Keep your letters in a private place and away from prying eyes. You don't want your words to be diluted or diminished by negative people. When I write my letters or make lists I always keep them private. People wonder how things always happen for me. My secret is to walk in silent power. I don't tell people what I'm doing but I allow the results to show for themselves. I'm sharing my techniques with you because I want you to use them to manifest what you want in your life. Just keep it to yourself! If people want to know how they can do what you've done, buy this book for them or send them the link to buy it for themselves.

List Writing
Listing what you want is just as powerful as writing letters. This is how I started my life of manifesting what I want. I made a simple list of all the things I wanted to happen in my life when my kids were small.

I've always been a to-do list maker which helped me stay on track, but making a goal list opened up more opportunities for me. I wasn't very intentionally at first, but when I found a list I made a prior year I was so excited. I made the list then put it in my desk drawer. I found the list when I was packing to move and was surprised to see that about 80% of the items on the list manifested. Amazing!!!

I started making more lists and I shared my techniques with my brother who told me a few months later how well the technique worked. Everything he wrote on the list manifested for him.

Later I read the book, *Write it Down Make it Happen*, and discovered that making a list is a top way people get their dreams and goals manifested. It's all about the intention you set when you write what you desire on paper.

Just remember that setting an intention is not the same as obsessing over how it is going to happen. It's not about worrying about it, stressing about it, or forcing things to happen. Putting in extra mental energy can potentially lower the vibration and discourage you.

Your Turn: So go ahead and write your letters and write your list so you can start seeing the things you want to manifest!

Pictures/Vision Board Manifestation

Writing is not the only way to manifest things. You can also manifest with pictures. Catherine Ponder wrote about creating a Wheel of Fortune which was basically a circle with spokes drawn in to divide the wheel into sections. The sections contain the areas of life you want to manifest your desire through pictures. It could include health, wealth, love, career, or anything that you want to see things happen.

Pictures are powerful because they help you see what you want. These pictures can be cut out from magazines, brochures, or any picture you find that represents what you want. When you find the pictures you want tape or glue them on a poster and hang it where you can see it daily. Each day, look at your board and say a word of thanks for everything on the list. Remember, gratitude is a powerful boost to manifesting what you desire.

You can put your pictures in other places including a collage you keep on your computer desktop, a binder full of images that represent what you want (remember the movie Last Holiday with Queen Latifah? She created this kind of binder), or you can create a mind movie (slide show) that you watch daily. Whichever way you choose to display your pictures, make sure you give thanks often.

My daughter used this method in a simplified yet powerful way to get into the university of her choice. She decided that she was going to go to Columbia University in NYC.

To make sure she remembered her goal she found a picture of the University and made it a wallpaper on her phone. I asked her why she had that picture and she told me it was because she wanted to remember her goal.

She applied for admission to the school and sent her transcripts and test scores. A few weeks later she got an email requesting a phone interview. The interview went well and then she waited. School would begin in a couple of weeks but she hadn't heard back yet but she had that picture.

Finally, a week before school started she got an email saying she was accepted! She also has everything paid for through her father's GI bill and she receives a stipend for living expenses.

She is blessed and living her best life because she held the vision (picture) of her goal on her phone's wallpaper.

Your Turn: Decide what you want. Next, find an image that represents your goal and put it on your phone's wallpaper then take inspired action.

Scripting Manifestation

I covered scripting earlier in this ebook. The scripting technique to manifest what you want involves writing a statement over and over on paper. The statement is what you desire written in future tense. For example, *I am thankful for the $10,000+ I receive in my bank account on Dec. 31, 2019.* This statement is a declaration of what you want to manifest.

Scripting is not just about writing the statement one time. You write the statement according to the number of days you plan to write. In other words, if you plan to write every day for three days to write the statement 33 times. If you plan to write every day for five days, write the statement 55 times. This is based on numerical signs 333 and 555. You might write for seven days 77 times. For more information on numerical signs, check out the various scripting YouTube videos online.

Writing your statements repeatedly impresses it on your subconscious mind. Your subconscious is connected to Spirit/Source/Universe who works to give you what you want. The repetition helps you focus on what you want, so it's always in the back of your mind so when it happens you recognize it.

From my story you saw that I wrote for two days to manifest money. I wrote two hundred times a day. You could say I made a concentrated effort. I had the time and motivation to write that much.

The awesome thing is that you may see the manifestation before you finish all of your days of writing. This depends on how deeply you feel and believe in the manifestation of your desire. Keep writing for the number of days you've committed to writing. When the manifestation comes, give thanks!

If you want many things to manifest in your life, script for one thing at a time to focus your energy. When the thing you desire manifests, move on to the next thing. Keep your vibration, belief, and gratitude high. This will open the way to greater manifestation. I'm so excited for you. The thing you desire will come!

Your Turn: Go to **Appendix A** to see the Scripting worksheets. Write your specific request on each line for your chosen number of days.

Two-Cup Manifestation

A new manifestation technique I learned about recently is the two-cup manifestation method. This technique is all about the power of negative to positive vibration transference combined with the spoken word. Basically, you are turning a negative situation into the positive situation you desire using positive vibration water.

To do the two-cup method you need a pen, paper, water, a candle, and two (preferably) glass drinking cups. Follow these steps:
1. Write your current situation on one piece of paper (sticky note) and write the situation you desire on another piece of paper
2. Light the candle and stick the current situation note on one glass and the desired situation on the other glass
3. Pour water into the current situation glass
4. Speak about the current situation turning into the desired situation
5. Pour the water into the desired situation glass
6. Speak prayer blessing and gratitude over the glass
7. Drink the water that has been blessed and give thanks!

After you have done the ritual, continue to give thanks and listen to music to keep your vibration high. Expect the desired situation to manifest at the right time. Each time you think about it, give thanks that the desired result is on the way. Otherwise forget about it and go on with your life.

I did this method when I wanted to feel reconnected to a loved one. Within 48 hours he contacted me and we talked more than we had ever talked. I felt reconnected to him and no longer felt upset and worried about the strained relationship. I plan to try this method again for other things.

Mirror Manifesting

The mirror technique is one of the more advanced techniques you can use to create your future. I teach this method to my relationship coaching clients. I'm sure you have heard the statement, "The eyes are the mirrors/windows of the soul". This is a true statement which is why the mirror technique is so powerful. Let me explain.

With the mirror method you go deeper into who you are as a person. You begin to confront yourself at the core. It is advanced because often people are not ready to confront themselves and the beliefs that have held them back from manifesting a better life. The mirror method helps you shift your mindset because you actually face your fears, your beliefs as stated before, and your deepest desires.

The mirror method helps you find your worthiness which is attached to what you manifest in your life. You can want good things to happen all day long but if your sense of worthiness or self-worth is small you will struggle with making your desires manifest.

The first step to mirror manifestation is getting to the core of yourself. Seeing who you truly are and inviting that person to come forward.

Warning: This technique will bring up some of your worst feelings and fears but if you are willing to push through you will break the curse of unworthiness.

Your Turn: Stand in front of a mirror and look yourself in the eyes. Stare at yourself and hold the gaze. Notice your eye color, the size of your pupils (dark part), then the white part.

Next look past the physical appearance of your eyes and begin to say kind words to yourself. *"You are a kind person. You are so smart. You did a great job with ____. You are such a good friend."* These self-appreciation comments are the first phase of the process. The next phase is all about expressing self-love which is a little more challenging. It was challenging for me when I first did it but I insisted and persisted with this exercise because I knew it would change my life. Are you ready?

Look in the mirror, into your eyes and say, *"I love you! I love you! I really love you! You are the greatest person in the world. You are so worthy of love; my love! I love you. I love you. I love you soooo much! You are the best things that ever happened to me. You are the best thing that ever happened to the world. You deserve the best!"*

Do this mirror technique every day for a week. Do it in the morning when you wake up and look in the mirror to wash your face or brush your teeth. After you do this for a week you will notice the change in how you feel about yourself. Your self-worth and self-esteem will soar. You will have new boundaries in your relationships, you will believe you deserve more than you have been accepting, you will be free from the fears that hold you back and you will be ready to manifest more than you could ever imagine.

The final phase of mirror manifestation is to tell yourself what you want in the mirror. Similar to the self-appreciation and self-love technique, the manifestation technique requires you to speak into your eyes the things you want.

Tell yourself you have XX amount of money, the trip to XX this year, the new job or job promotion, or whatever you want. Follow it with, *"I am worthy and it is so"*. To follow up, speak words of thanks for the thing you want. Say, *"I'm so thankful for the job at XX or job promotion. I'm so thankful for XX amount of money. I'm so thankful for the trip to XX this year."*

Saying thank you for what you desire is a huge part of manifesting. You are acting as if or feeling it real.

EFT Manifestation

EFT or Emotional Freedom Technique is a method I've used to change many things in my life that held me back from experiencing a life of manifestation. You may be wondering what does emotional freedom have to do with manifesting? It actually has a lot to do with manifesting because emotions feed our feelings. Feelings are just another form or energy or vibration coming from us which allows or blocks our manifestations.

If our emotions are stuck in low feeling vibrations it is hard to manifest the good things we desire. I grew up around sad, angry, depressed people so I felt sad, angry, and depressed. I had almost zero coping and problem solving skills. I felt stuck in this cycle of low vibration emotions. I rarely saw anyone around me happy, excited, or seeing their dreams come true. I didn't know it was possible to feel anything other than sadness on a consistent basis.

I spent years trying to understand and change my personality, temperament, and idiosyncrasies but it didn't help me be happier. If anything, I became more depressed and hopeless. I felt deep in my soul that there was a solution.

I came across EFT in my research to heal my depression. A man named Gary Craig pioneered a technique he called emotional acupuncture, later named EFT. By **tapping certain points on the body's energy meridians** the emotions would be released and your life could be changed.

I began using this technique to heal my depression and unblock my emotions. I went from stuck in low vibration feelings to a normal range of emotions/feelings and being able to control them as well as use them to manifest what I needed and wanted in life.

EFT is not only good for unblocking emotions but also good for manifesting the things you desire. The question is how? EFT involves tapping on a set up statement (similar to what you do in scripting) on the side of the hand, then tapping through the other points with an anchor word or phrase.

EFT Tapping Points

- SH: side of hand
- TH: top of head
- EB: eyebrow
- SE: side of eye
- UE: under eye
- UN: under nose
- CP: chin
- SS: sore spot
- CB: collarbone
- UA: under arm 4" below

www.theartoftapping.com
Copyright © Patricia Fenbe 2017

For example, if I want to manifest a good grade on a test I would set it up with the phrase, "I'm thankful I passed my Math test even though feel test anxiety." Say this phrase three times tapping on the side of the hand. Next say I pass the test while tapping on each point on your body (see the diagram) for two or three rounds. Take a deep breath after each round.

You should feel a sense of calm after you finish tapping. You may also find yourself yawning which is an indication that any blocked emotions have cleared. Go about your day feeling excited and grateful for passing the test.

Your Turn: Watch this [YouTube video](#) to learn how to do the EFT steps. Once you know how to do the steps apply it to a desire you want to manifest.

Feeling it Real is the Secret

At the core of each technique is about feeling it real just as Law of Attraction expert, Neville Goddard advises. If you have never heard of Neville Goddard, he is one person you want to get familiar with. The easiest way to learn about his methods is to watch/listen to his videos on YouTube. There are several videos posted with his live lectures and excerpts from his books.

Feeling it real is about using your imagination to make your desires come true. When we imagine things we put ourselves in the picture and see it from the inside out. We are looking at the picture in our mind, we are hearing the voices, we are feeling the feelings associated with the imagination. It's like we are creating a film of our lives the way we want to see it happen.

When I was a teen I did this technique often. I didn't really understand it or know there was a name for it. For instance, I would imagine I worked at a certain company. I would see myself entering the building and sitting at my desk doing work. Sometimes it was a flash in my mind or I would spend 5-7 minutes seeing this happen.

Later I learned how powerful this technique was so when I wanted a job I would see myself getting the phone call that I got the job, I would hear the words, Congratulations you got the job!

I know my thoughts are powerful and I want you to know this too. You can have ANYTHING you want when you are specific and decisive.

Final Thoughts

The manifestation techniques described in this book only work if you put in the effort to both understand and take action. If you choose to put this book away and not take action you will not see the results you've been wishing for. But I can guarantee the person who does take action will see results.

Cultivate Your Confidence

When I was younger (before I had children) I believed I could have anything I wanted. I was confident about this despite my background. This confidence came from deep within me. I prayed for wisdom. I watched my dad hone his craft and work with confidence; so much confidence in his ability that he had no fear of losing his job because with his tools and his knowledge he could get a job anywhere. I believe this is partly where my confidence came from. Believing I could have anything I want in the world helps me manifest the things I want.

Obey the Law of Giving and Receiving

Many people make the mistake of believing manifesting is only about receiving. This is only part of the law of attraction. The other part is giving. Giving and receiving goes hand in hand. Without one you will struggle to have the other. But once you begin to regularly give you will see that you will receive more than you hoped or imagined. I like to think of it as a cycle of giving, receiving, and being grateful. I call it the

Gratitude Cycle. The more you give the more you receive the more you have to be grateful for then the more you want to give and on and on and on. Never be afraid to give because giving is simply a seed you are planting for the future.

Have you ever heard of a farmer eating all the seeds he needs to plant? He would never have a harvest if he did that. So you must follow the example of the farmer and start planting seeds of money, time, and talents.

Whatever you want is what you should plant. Want more money? Plant more money seeds. What more time? Plant more time-seed. Want more talents? Plant more talents.

When you plant your seeds (give) you and trust that you will receive back 10x, 100x, or even 1,000x more. You are banking on your future with the seeds you plant. Just be sure to keep the cycle going or else your seed will rot because you've hoarded it.

The ABCs of Prayer

Prayer is a powerful tool to use when you are manifesting a life you love. Prayer has many functions including, acknowledging the Creator and Source of everything, speaking what you want into existence, and encouraging yourself.

Prayer can happen anywhere so you don't have to get on your knees, lay face down on the floor, or moan and groan. It can be done when you are working, cooking, driving, laying in bed, or walking in nature. Prayer is simply a conversation, meditation, and listening. It is a powerful tool in your manifestation arsenal

You may be wondering what are the ABCs of prayer? It is **A**sking, **B**elieving, and **C**laiming.

Asking - This seems obvious especially since asking is what the book is all about. However, as you also learned there are ways to ask for what you want that are more advantageous than others. For instance, asking with excitement and anticipation is better than asking in fear and trepidation. The latter will stop an answer to prayer in their tracks. Yikes!

Believing - Believing for something can be tough. We don't exactly live in a world of trust and openness. But belief is essential in prayer and in manifesting what you desire. When you believe in what you are asking for you are essentially practicing faith. Faith means you can see the thing you desire in your mind before you feel it in your hands. If you don't think your are very good at having faith or believing you are mistaken. You have faith each time you drive in your city, step out of your house, or eat food from a restaurant. You have faith alright, you just have to extend it to the things you are asking for.

Claiming - This might seem a bit odd when it comes to prayer but it fits right in. You can ask and you can believe but until you claim what is yours (the thing you asked for) you may be waiting longer than needed. It's like asking for an ice cream cone, imagining how good it will taste, but never accepting it after you've paid for it. You have to actually reach for what you want. So claim what you want when you see the answer to prayer.

Prayer is indeed powerful and you can use it to receive what you deeply desire when you know how to use it correctly/ effectively.

Want Additional Support?
Can you honestly commit to trying this technique on your next goal?

Do you have the support and accountability you need to see it through to the end?

What kind of distractions will you allow to get in the way?

Do you think you could benefit from being a member of a Manifestation Mastermind group?

Would it be great to be a part of a group of like-minded people who will encourage you and keep you accountable?

It would be my pleasure to create this kind of space for you, however I only want to do it for people who would take full advantage of it rather than let it be another ghost town Facebook group.

Please <u>complete this survey</u> and let me know that you are interested in individual coaching.

Resources for Manifesting Money

Books on Amazon.com

7 Habits of Highly Effective People

It Works

Write it Down Make it Happen

Accidental Genius: Using Writing to Generate Your Best Ideas, Insight, and Content

Money, Manifestations & Miracles: 8 Principles for Transforming Women's Relationship with Money

Get Rich, Lucky Bitch!: Release Your Money Blocks and Live a First Class Life

MONEY Master the Game: 7 Simple Steps to Financial Freedom

Appendix A - Scripting Worksheets
55 x 5 Worksheet

Print five sets of the worksheets for each day. Write your desire in a present tense statement on each line below for five days.

1.	
2.	
3.	
4.	
5.	
6.	
7.	
8.	
9.	
10.	
11.	
12.	
13.	
14.	
15.	
16.	

17.
18.
19.
20.
21.
22.
23.
24.
25.
26.
27.
28.
29.
30.
31.
32.
33.
34.
35.
36.
37.

38.
39.
40.
41.
42.
43.
44.
45.
46.
47.
48.
49.
50.
51.
52.
53.
54.
55.

33 x 3 Worksheet

Print three sets of the worksheets for each day. Write your desire in a present tense statement on each line below for three days.

1.	
2.	
3.	
4.	
5.	
6.	
7.	
8.	
9.	
10.	
11.	
12.	
13.	
14.	
15.	
16.	
17.	

| 18. |
| 19. |
| 20. |
| 21. |
| 22. |
| 23. |
| 24. |
| 25. |
| 26. |
| 27. |
| 28. |
| 29. |
| 30. |
| 31. |
| 32. |
| 33. |

Appendix B - Sexy Good Goals Worksheet

Each new day holds unlimited potential. How will you use it? Will you harness the potential and bend it to your will or will you let it go to waste?

A proven way to get what you want out of life is to write down your goals. It can be overwhelming to think about because the possibilities are endless. Trying to boil the ocean is impossible so let's scoop out a small amount and boil it instead.

How?

Think about your general goals and then break it down into manageable pieces.

Most people want to
- Be rich
- Travel
- Be healthy
- Go to/ finish school
- Get a new car
- Buy a house
-Get married
- Start a business

These are all general goals most people have. They are vague and have no date attached. In essence they are dreams. Let's get specific about these dreams and tailor them to you.

On the next few pages you can create goals through a series of questions designed to help you write powerful, actionable goals. Let's get started!

In the space below answer the questions. At the end of the worksheet you will have your 3-5 goals for the week.

1. List your general goals *(example: Lose weight)*

_____

_____

_____

_____

_____

2. What do you want to accomplish with the dreams you've written? (Write one line sentences)
    Fit in size 8 dress

_____

_____

_____

_____

_____

3. When do you want to finish the goal?

    By this summer

_____

_____

_____

_____

_____

4. What steps do you need to take? What is the process?

(Research if you need to)

Eat healthier low carb high protein meals and walk 30 minutes daily

_____

_____

_____

_____

5. Combine questions 2-4 in an "I am" statement.

I am a size 8 by this summer because I eat low carb high protein meals and walk 30 minutes every day.

_____

_____

_____

_____

_____

Now you have a goal you can reach because it is specific and has a date. You know what you are working towards, when you will accomplish it, and the end results.

Do this for all your dreams. There are a few logical steps you must take to reach the ultimate goal you have so do your research, ask questions, take action.

Your goal statement should look like this:

I am/have _____ by _____ because I _____ and _____ every _____.

Now you have created your own sexy good goals. Now put them where you can see them on a daily basis. Stick them on your bathroom mirror, on the back of your door, in your car, on your computer screen. You can even make it your screensaver! No matter where you put your goals, make sure you read it each day and think about it before you go to sleep at night. You will soon see that your goals are becoming reality.

_____

www.ingramcontent.com/pod-product-compliance
Lightning Source LLC
LaVergne TN
LVHW051203080426
835508LV00021B/2779